Owl

Nick Winnick

AV2

www.av2books.com

Step 1
Go to **www.av2books.com**

Step 2
Enter this unique code

RDMTND1KR

Step 3
Explore your interactive eBook!

CONTENTS

AV2 is optimized for use on any device

Your interactive eBook comes with...

Contents
Browse a live contents page to easily navigate through resources

Audio
Listen to sections of the book read aloud

Videos
Watch informative video clips

Weblinks
Gain additional information for research

Try This!
Complete activities and hands-on experiments

Key Words
Study vocabulary, and complete a matching word activity

Quizzes
Test your knowledge

Slideshows
View images and captions

... and much, much more!

Contents

Meet the Owl

Owls are common birds, but they are not always easy to spot. This is because most owls are nocturnal. They are most active at night and sleep during the day. During an Arctic summer, it is light out much of the time. This is why some owls are active in the day as well as at night.

Owls have special body features that make them better suited to hunting at night. For example, they are silent fliers, so **prey** cannot hear them. Also, their feathers often match the coloring of their surroundings. This helps keep owls from being seen.

The width of a bird's wings, when they are spread out from tip to tip, is called its wingspan. Snowy owls have a wingspan of 54 to 65 inches (137 to 165 centimeters).

Eagle owls are the **largest** owls. They can have wingspans of **6.6 feet**. (2 meters)

Where Owls Live

Owls can be found in nearly every country on Earth. The great horned owl has a vast **range**. These owls live throughout North America and South America.

Owls have a wide variety of **habitats**. Barn owls hunt in open fields, grasslands, and sparse woodlands. Snowy owls can be found in boreal forests and Arctic **tundras**.

 Great horned owls have one of the best-known hoots. Their "whoohoo-ho-o-o" can be heard in natural areas across the United States.

Owls in North America

Owls can be found on every continent, except Antarctica. There are about 200 different **species** of owls living today. Of these, about 19 owl species live in North America.

Greenland

Canada

Northwest Territories

Nunavut

British Columbia

Alberta

Saskatchewan

Manitoba

Ontario

Quebec

Newfoundland and Labrador

New Brunswick

Prince Edward Island

United States

Washington

Montana

North Dakota

Minnesota

Maine

Oregon

Idaho

Wyoming

South Dakota

Wisconsin

Michigan

Nova Scotia

New Hampshire

Vermont

Massachusetts

Rhode Island

Connecticut

New Jersey

New York

Nevada

Utah

Colorado

Nebraska

Iowa

Illinois

Indiana

Ohio

Pennsylvania

California

Arizona

New Mexico

Kansas

Missouri

Kentucky

West Virginia

Virginia

Delaware

Maryland

Oklahoma

Arkansas

Tennessee

North Carolina

South Carolina

Texas

Louisiana

Mississippi

Alabama

Georgia

Mexico

Florida

Pacific Ocean

Atlantic Ocean

Hawai'i

Scale

125 Miles

0   125 Kilometers

Legend

- ■ Owl Habitat
- ▢ Water

Scale

250 Miles

0   250 Kilometers

N E S W

Owl History

Modern birds developed from a group of dinosaurs called theropods. Theropods first appeared about 230 million years ago. Some well-known theropods are the *Velociraptor* and *Tyrannosaurus rex*.

Some small theropods grew feathers to keep warm. Over time, they grew muscles and longer feathers to help them fly. This group of theropods survived when all other dinosaurs became **extinct** about 65 million years ago. Over time, they developed into the birds that live today.

One of the **first** feathered dinosaur fossils was found in **1861**. It belonged to a dinosaur known as archeopteryx.

A group of owls is called a parliament, a word that is also used to describe a group of government officials. Owls were thought to be wise by some cultures.

Owl Shelter

Owls live in many different places. Some owls take shelter in towering forests. Others make their homes in hollows in the ground.

Great horned owls live far from human settlements. They make their homes in dense woodlands, and along cliffs and canyons. Burrowing owls live on prairies and open plains. They nest in burrows made by badgers, ground squirrels, and other digging animals.

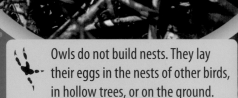

Owls do not build nests. They lay their eggs in the nests of other birds, in hollow trees, or on the ground.

Owls find different places to sleep, depending on the species and their surroundings. Common places are hollow trees, burrows, and rafters in farm buildings.

Owl Features

Owls have special **adaptations** that help them hunt well at night. For example, owls have large eyes. This lets them take in as much light as possible to improve their night vision. Owls' eyes face forward to help them judge distances.

NECK

Since owls cannot move their eyes, they must turn their head to change their view. An owl's neck can turn 270 degrees to either side. This lets them look almost directly behind their body.

WINGS AND FEATHERS

Many owls have broad wings that let them glide easily. Owl feathers have tiny bristles on their front edges. This muffles the sound they make while flying, letting owls move silently.

EARS

An owl's ears point forward. They have large openings that are surrounded by feathers. This makes them more sensitive to sounds. Owls use their hearing to help them catch prey.

EYES

Owls are farsighted. They have difficulty seeing objects that are too close to their faces. They can see well at night and in daylight.

BEAK AND TALONS

Owls have hook-shaped beaks that curve downward. They also have sharp, curved **talons** at the end of each of their four toes. Both the beak and talons are used to catch and tear prey.

What Do Owls Eat?

Owls are birds of prey. They hunt small animals for food. One of the most impressive hunters is the great horned owl. These owls prey mainly on rabbits, grouse, and ducks. They have also been known to hunt geese, skunks, and even porcupines.

Some strong owls tear up large prey before eating it. However, many owls swallow their food whole. Soft parts of the prey are **digested**. Bones, teeth, fur, and feathers are coughed up in bunches known as pellets.

Many farmers raise barn owls. They are used to control rats, mice, and shrews that eat crops.

Owls are a large group of birds with many different kinds of prey. However, their main diet is made up of rodents.

Owl Life Cycle

Owls have many ways of attracting mates and raising their young. Most owls attract mates with their calls and their feathers. In some species, males will offer females a gift of food. A male and female owl will remain together for life.

Eggs

A mated pair of owls stays together to look after their eggs. Often, the male will hunt, while the female keeps the eggs warm. In some species, these roles are shared. After about two weeks to two months of nesting, the eggs will hatch.

Adults

Most owls are ready to mate about one year after hatching. In nature, owls' life spans vary greatly. Barn owls typically only live to be 1 or 2 years old. However, great horned owls can live as long as 13 years in nature and more than 30 years in **captivity**.

Once a pair of owls have mated, they look for a safe place to lay their eggs. Some owls, such as the great horned owl, only lay one egg at a time. Other species may lay as many as 12. Most lay three or four.

Owlets

A newly hatched owl is called an owlet. Most owlets can fly about a month after hatching. By 2 months old, owlets leave the nesting spot to begin hunting. At as early as 4 months old, owlets are strong fliers and powerful hunters.

Encountering Owls

Owls are not known for harming humans. However, they can be dangerous. It is best to keep a safe distance from them. Disturbing a sleeping or nesting owl could frighten the bird. Great horned owls, for example, can be aggressive when guarding their eggs. They may try to defend themselves.

Shaking trees, shining lights, and making owl calls are common ways to upset these animals. Such upsets can cause changes to their way of life. They may be unable to hunt and feed their babies as they normally would. This can be harmful to the owls.

Great gray owls have a **third eyelid**. It protects their eyes from small objects when they attack prey.

A pair of binoculars lets people get a good look at owls without disturbing them.

Myths and Legends

Owls are important in cultures around the world. People in almost every country have stories about them. An owl might be a symbol of good or bad luck, death, or wisdom.

At one time, people in India would count the hoots of owls to gain clues about the future. One hoot was a symbol of death. Two hoots was a sign of good luck. Three hoots meant there soon would be a wedding in the family.

In ancient Greece, the goddess of wisdom, Athena, was often shown with an owl. To this day, owls are a symbol of wisdom to many people.

Harry and Hedwig

Some cultures believe that owls have mystical powers. Owls are often involved in stories of sorcery and magic. For example, owls are an important part of the Harry Potter series of books and movies, where they act as messengers. In the wizarding world, owls are prized for their wisdom and skill at finding people. Harry Potter has a snowy owl named Hedwig.

Although Hedwig is a female owl in the story, she is played by male owls in the films. Male snowy owls are nearly pure white, like the one in the movie. Females have dark bands across the chest and wings. Using a male snowy owl to play Hedwig made it easier for the actors to carry the bird. This is because most male owls weigh slightly less than females.

Quiz

1 What makes up an owl's main diet?

2 When did theropods first appear?

3 Which Greek goddess was often shown with an owl?

4 What is the largest type of owl?

5 Which continent is not home to owls?

6 How many toes do owls have?

7 What is a group of owls called?

8 How many eggs do most owl species lay?

ANSWERS
1. Rodents **2.** About 230 million years ago **3.** Athena **4.** The eagle owl **5.** Antarctica **6.** Four **7.** A parliament **8.** Three or four

Key Words

adaptations: changes that make an animal better suited to different conditions

captivity: not living in a natural habitat

digested: broken down by the body and used for nourishment

extinct: an entire species of animals with no living members

habitats: natural living places

prey: animals that are hunted by other animals for food

range: the area over which an animal travels in search of food

species: animals or plants that share certain features and can breed together

talons: sharp claws found on certain birds

tundras: arctic plains with small plants and frozen ground

Index

Get the best
of both worlds.

AV2 bridges the gap between print and digital.

The expandable resources toolbar enables quick access to content including **videos**, **audio**, **activities**, **weblinks**, **slideshows**, **quizzes**, and **key words**.

Animated videos make static images come alive.

Resource icons on each page help readers to further **explore key concepts**.

Published by AV2
350 5th Avenue, 59th Floor
New York, NY 10118
Website: www.av2books.com

Library of Congress Control Number: 2019955112
ISBN 978-1-7911-2083-2 (hardcover)
ISBN 978-1-7911-2084-9 (softcover)
ISBN 978-1-7911-2085-6 (multi-user eBook)
ISBN 978-1-7911-2086-3 (single-user eBook)

Printed in Guangzhou, China
1 2 3 4 5 6 7 8 9 0   24 23 22 21 20

022020
101119

Editor: Katie Gillespie
Designer: Ana María Vidal

Every reasonable effort has been made to trace ownership and to obtain permission to reprint copyright material. The publishers would be pleased to have any errors or omissions brought to their attention so that they may be corrected in subsequent printings.

AV2 acknowledges Getty Images, Alamy, Minden Pictures, iStock, and Shutterstock as its primary image suppliers for this title.